HIP-HOP

Hip-Hop

Mary J. Blige

Terrell Brown

Mason Crest Publishers

Mary J. Blige

FRONTIS After a rough patch in her personal and professional lives, Mary J. Blige has returned to the top of the hip-hop scene.

PRODUCED BY 21ST CENTURY PUBLISHING AND COMMUNICATIONS, INC.

EDITORIAL BY HARDING HOUSE PUBLISHING SERVICES, INC.

MASON CREST PUBLISHERS INC.
370 Reed Road
Broomall, Pennsylvania 19008
(866)MCP-BOOK (toll free)
www.masoncrest.com

Printed in Malaysia.

9 8 7 6 5 4 3 2

Library of Congress Cataloging-in-Publication Data

Brown, Terrell.
    Mary J. Blige / by Terrell Brown.
        p. cm. — (Hip-hop)
    Includes index.
    ISBN 1-4222-0113-9
    1. Blige, Mary J. 2. Rap musicians—UnitedStates—Biography—Juvenile literature.
    I. Title. II. Series.
    ML3930.B585B76 2007
    782.421643092—dc22
    [B]   2006012650

Contents

Hip-Hop Timeline

1974 Hip-hop pioneer Afrika Bambaataa organizes the Universal Zulu Nation.

1988 *Yo! MTV Raps* premieres on MTV.

1970s Hip-hop as a cultural movement begins in the Bronx, New York City.

1985 *Krush Groove*, a hip-hop film about Def Jam Recordings, is released featuring Run-D.M.C., Kurtis Blow, LL Cool J, and the Beastie Boys.

1970s DJ Kool Herc pioneers the use of breaks, isolations, and repeats using two turntables.

1979 The Sugarhill Gang's song "Rapper's Delight" is the first hip-hop single to go gold.

1986 Run-D.M.C. are the first rappers to appear on the cover of *Rolling Stone* magazine.

1970

1980

1988

1976 Grandmaster Flash & the Furious Five pioneer hip-hop MCing and freestyle battles.

1986 Beastie Boys' album *Licensed to Ill* is released and becomes the best-selling rap album of the 1980s.

1970s Break dancing emerges at parties and in public places in New York City.

1982 Afrika Bambaataa embarks on the first European hip-hop tour.

1988 Hip-hop music annual record sales reaches $100 million.

1970s Graffiti artist Vic pioneers tagging on subway trains in New York City.

1984 *Graffiti Rock*, the first hip-hop television program, premieres.

6

1993 Rapper Snoop Dogg's album *Doggystyle* is the first debut album to hit the music charts at number one.

2006 Queen Latifah becomes the first hip-hop artist to receive a star on the Hollywood Walk of Fame.

1989 DJ Jazzy Jeff & The Fresh Prince become the first hip-hop artists to win a Grammy Award.

2003 Rapper Eminem becomes the first hip-hop artist to win an Academy Award.

2005 Hip-hop artist Kanye West appears on the cover of *Time* magazine.

1989 Rap is added as a new category to the *Billboard* charts.

1997 East Coast rapper Notorious B.I.G. (aka Biggie Smalls) is murdered.

2004 First National Hip-Hop Political Convention is held in Newark, New Jersey.

1989   2000   2006

1990s Hip-hop emerges in Europe.

1996 West Coast rapper Tupac Shakur is shot and killed.

2005 Rapper Will Smith opens the Philadelphia Live 8 concert as part of 10 simultaneous concerts held worldwide to bring attention to the extreme poverty in Africa.

1989 First gangsta rap album, *Straight Outta Compton*, is released by N.W.A.

2001 The hip-hop political action group, Hip-Hop Summit Action Network, is founded by Russell Simmons.

2006 The Smithsonian Institute National Museum of American History announces the creation of a new hip-hop exhibition scheduled to open in three to five years.

1992 Dr. Dre's album *The Chronic* is released; it redefines West Coast rap.

In 2002, Mary J. Blige told the story of her personal pain to the world through the song "No More Drama." That album brought her a Grammy nomination. To Mary, it's more than a title, though; it's her goal for the rest of her life.

1

The Queen Looks Backward

On the evening of February 27, 2002, Mary J. Blige shimmered in gold lamé as she went on stage for the televised Grammy Award ceremony. At first her voice was quiet and gentle as she sang her hit song, "No More Drama." The **R&B** ballad spoke frankly of her personal pain and perseverance.

"No more pain, no more drama in my life, no more drama make me hurt again," Mary crooned. But halfway through the song, her genuine emotion—all the tears and rage and courage that her life had demanded—seemed to take over her voice. Instead of offering the polished, glittering production typical of a Grammy performance, Mary sang with an utter and stunning honesty, laying herself bare to the worldwide audience of millions. She crouched down, then leapt up; she ran back and forth; she tossed her head like a wild horse; and several times, she seemed so overcome with feeling that she almost lost her balance and toppled to the floor.

When the song finally came to an end, the audience seemed stunned by Mary's naked passion—but Mary herself looked as though she were near tears. After all, she knew how hard she had worked to get to the Grammys—and she knew all the anguish and heartache she had endured.

A Queen Is Born in the Projects

Thanks to Mary's hit albums, she has earned the title "Queen of Hip-Hop Soul"—however, the circumstances of her early life were far from luxurious or royal.

She was born in the Bronx on January 11, 1971, the youngest of Cora and Thomas Blige's two daughters. Her father was a jazz musician, but he left the family before his youngest daughter's fourth birthday. After her divorce, Cora took Mary and her older sister, LaTonya, to their grandmother's home in Savannah, Georgia. There, Cora pulled herself together and returned to the Bronx before Mary turned five. She did the best she could to raise her girls on her own.

Life was hard for the Blige girls. After a couple of years, they moved out of the Bronx to nearby Yonkers, where they settled in the Schlobam Housing Projects. Because of the apartment buildings' reputation for crime and drugs, they were also known as "Slow Bam." Living there meant that danger and violence were everyday facts of life. Years later, on *The Oprah Winfrey Show*, Mary revealed that she was sexually assaulted during these years.

Mary described her growing up years to *Essence* magazine:

> **"Every day I would be getting into fights over whatever. You always had to prove yourself to keep from getting robbed or jumped. Growing up in the projects is like living in a barrel of crabs. If you try to get out, one of the other crabs tries to pull you down."**

Eventually, music became Mary's refuge, the place where she could escape from the tension and violence all around her. She sang lead in her church's choir—and at seven, she won a talent contest singing Aretha Franklin's "Respect."

With their mother working long hours, LaTonya had to be "the mommy" in the Blige household. She ironed the clothes, cooked the food, looked after Mary—and occasionally even gave her a spanking or

Music was Mary's outlet during a difficult childhood. When she was just seven, she won a talent contest singing "Respect," by the legendary Aretha Franklin. In 2001, Mary had the chance to perform with the music diva.

two if LaTonya felt her little sister wasn't behaving the way she ought. Both little girls had to grow up fast. Mary told *Essence*, "It's like I was old when I was young."

Family life didn't offer Mary a lot of comfort or **affirmation**. Years later, when she was an adult, in an interview with *The Guardian*, she described some of the emotional scars she suffered at the hands of her family:

> **"The environment that I was in—they'll be mad at me, but it's the truth—they were angry, hateful, jealous, ignorant, prideful people. My aunts were very, very mean people. I didn't want to be like that.**

But it turns out that everything I didn't want to be like, that's what I ended up being like. . . . Whatever I do, I came from that. I came from that tree."

Her extended family predicted nothing but bad for Mary. She'd never finish high school, they said. She'd never amount to anything. She'd end up in trouble. Even if she did something good, they never acted proud of her. Her family—in fact, her entire community— seemed like a trap she could never escape.

Life didn't get any easier for Mary as she entered her teen years. As a release from her life's tensions, she began experimenting with drugs, and in the eleventh grade, she dropped out of school (fulfilling her aunts' predictions). Her friends on the street were as rough as she was, and she ended up with a scar on her face from a knife fight. She earned what money she could working as a babysitter, a hairdresser, and a telephone operator. Basically, though, she was going nowhere fast, just like her family had always said she would.

Music was still the one safe place she knew, the one place where she could be honest and feel good about herself. Her mother's choice in music—Donny Hathaway, Otis Redding, and Gladys Knight— influenced her own style, but Mary also loved the sound of hip-hop.

Growing Up with Hip-Hop

Hip-hop was born about the same time as Mary, right there in the same place where she was born, in New York City's Bronx. No wonder then that hip-hop was in Mary's blood. Years later, she told BallerStatus.net:

"At the end of the day, hip-hop is the foundation of Mary J. Blige. Hip-hop is the reason why my music even exists. I wouldn't have a bed of music [without it]. . . . I'm never going to resent or disrespect it. When I rise, it rises. . . . It's a part of Mary J. Blige."

Hip-hop is more than just music—it also includes its own styles of art, dance, speech, and fashion. Rap—hip-hop's rhyming, rhythmic music—has its roots deep in African culture and oral tradition. The earliest African Americans listened to the echo of their homeland, whether they were worshipping or working, and they had fun with words, using rhyme and rhythm to praise God, complain about their work, or play rhyming, clapping games. From churchgoers to prison labor gangs, from schoolchildren to grandmas and grandpas, down through the years, African Americans liked to rap. They liked to beat out rhythms with sticks and hands and homemade drums; they liked to move their bodies to that rhythm; and they liked to fit words together in patterns that rhymed and jumped right along with beat of their hands and the jiggle of their bodies.

Modern-day rap music came to life in the early 1970s, when a Jamaican **DJ** known as Kool Herc tried to use his island style of DJing—which involved reciting **improvised** rhymes over **dubbed**

Mary and hip-hop were born about the same time. Both have grown up to be responsible citizens of the world. Here, left to right, Reverend Run, Mary, Ludacris, Roberta Shields, C. Virginia Fields, and Russell Simmons appear at an awards dinner for Hip-Hop Summit Action Network (HSAN) in 2004.

What began in the streets of the Bronx is now in history books and museums. In 2006, Kool Herc, one of hip-hop's founders, was a special guest at a press conference announcing the first Hip-Hop Exhibition at the Smithsonian National Museum of American History.

versions of his **reggae** records—at parties in the Bronx. New Yorkers weren't into reggae back then, though, so Kool Herc adapted his style by chanting over the instrumental or percussion sections of the day's popular songs. Because these instrumental and percussion breaks were relatively short, he learned to extend them indefinitely by using an audio **mixer** and two identical records to continuously replay the desired segment. Rap took off from there.

The hip-hop culture—which also includes graffiti street art and break dancing—gave young urban New Yorkers something they desperately needed at a time when prejudice, poverty, and unemployment were their only realities: a chance to express themselves, a way to feel good about themselves. Rap was an art form anyone could do. You didn't need a lot of money or expensive instruments to rhyme. You didn't need to take lessons. Rapping could be practiced any time, anywhere.

Today, rap is still a form of self-expression that's within urban kids' reach. By the twenty-first century, however, hip-hop has become a whole lot more than just something street kids do; it has grown into a multimillion-dollar business. At the same time, it is still doing what African American music has always done—speaking out on behalf of the black community.

This is the positive side of hip-hop music, the side that's **democratic**, honest, and creative. Unfortunately, like most everything to do with

In the early days of hip-hop, the turntable and DJ were its most important "musical" performers. One of the early pioneers was Grandmaster Flash, seen here at the 31st Anniversary of Hip-Hop Culture in 2005.

Surrounded by poverty, violence, and drugs, Mary turned to hip-hop as a way to express herself—her pain and her anger—and as a way out of her circumstances. Fans could relate to her story, and they were generous with their love.

human beings, there's also a negative side. Plenty of people don't like hip-hop because they say it encourages violence, bad language, and just plain old rudeness.

Truth is, quite a few hip-hop musicians *have* been involved with violence. Death Row Records producer Marion "Suge" Knight served five years for assault and federal weapons violations. 50 Cent was arrested for hiding assault weapons in his car. In 2000, at least five different fights broke out at the Source Hiphop Awards, and the final brawl was so big that it shut the ceremony down. A few hip-hop musicians have even been murdered, including Tupac Shakur, Biggie Smalls, and Jam Master Jay. What's more, a certain kind of hip-hop, called "gangsta rap," focuses on violence, drugs, and disrespect for women.

Some people defend even this style of rap, though; they say that at least it's honest. And although some Americans would rather hide their heads from the truth, hip-hop calls it like it is: the poverty in America's cities tends to breed violence, drug abuse, and promiscuous sex. That's just the way things are. Refusing to look at it or speak of it won't make it go away. As the classic hip-hop artist Grandmaster Flash wrote in his 1982 hit "The Message": "You grow in the ghetto, living second rate/And your eyes will sing a song of deep hate."

Hip-hop music is often controversial, no doubt about it. At the same time, many people around the world—including **sociologists** and literary critics, as well as musicians—continue to admire hip-hop's **brazen** courage and cultural integrity. Hip-hop music gives a powerful voice to a huge population of **marginalized** people who would otherwise be powerless and voiceless.

And that's what it did for Mary J. Blige. At a time in her life when circumstances had combined to teach her that she had no options, no self-worth, and no skills, hip-hip allowed her to shout to the world her pain and rage.

And to her surprise, the world listened.

Mary's career began with a win at a talent show when she was seven and a demo tape cut on a lark at seventeen. Though she made the demo as a joke, her rendition of "Caught Up in the Rapture" caught the attention of a record executive.

2

Pain and Soul

One afternoon, when Mary was seventeen, she and some friends were hanging out at a local shopping mall. Just for kicks, her friends persuaded her to cut a demo tape at a recording booth. Mary sang Anita Baker's "Caught Up in the Rapture." And then she didn't give her **impromptu** performance much further thought.

But her mother was impressed with the way Mary sounded on tape, so Cora gave the demo to her boyfriend. Eventually, the boyfriend played the cassette for someone he knew in the music industry, Jeff Redd, a recording artist and A&R runner for Uptown Records. (A&R stands for "artists and repertoire"—and an A&R runner is basically a talent scout who seeks out new artists for a recording company.)

An Open Door

Redd sent the tape to Uptown's president, Andre Harrell. At the time, Uptown was a relatively new label, with a few noted hip-hop and R&B

musicians already signed, including Heavy D and Guy. Harrell liked what he heard on the amateur tape.

He told *Essence*:

> **"When I first heard Mary's voice, I heard all the pain and soul, and I knew she had something important. Her interpretation of soul has given women in the inner city pride. She took the girl from around the way and made her something cool to be."**

Harrell met with Mary, and in 1989, she became the company's youngest artist—and its first female musician.

After signing with Uptown, however, not a whole lot changed for Mary, at least not right away. The label was focusing most of its time and money on more established musicians. Two years went by before Mary got her first assignment: she sang the hook on "I'll Do 4 U" by rapper Father MC, and she also was a backup singer on the song's music video.

Mary may have been disappointed that things weren't moving faster—but she hadn't had a lot of expectations to start with. And whether she knew it or not, a door had opened for her, a door that would lead her out of the projects forever. At this point, maybe that doorway was still only cracked open, but soon it would swing wide.

What's the 411?

Finally, early in 1992, Uptown gave the green light to the production of Mary's **debut** album, *What's the 411?* The album's title came from one of Mary's past jobs: a directory assistance operator. Harrell assigned Mary to his rising executive, Sean "Puffy" Combs, who would oversee the project. Harrell also enlisted some of the leading R&B and hip-hop producers of the time, including Tony Dofat, Mark Morales (who had brought the Fat Boys to fame), Mark C. Rooney, Dave "Jam" Hall, and DeVanté Swing.

Swing was also a member of another Uptown act, Jodeci. Mary's professional association with Swing led to an introduction with another Jodeci member, K-Ci Hailey. Mary and K-Ci were attracted to each other, and they embarked on a long-term relationship. Through the months that followed, as Mary's career climbed steadily upward, her relationship with K-Ci also went up sometimes—but just as often, it took emotional plunges that left Mary reeling.

In 1989, Uptown Records' president Andre Harrell signed the young Mary to her first recording contract. Though it took a while, this was the beginning of Mary's path to success and out of the desperate conditions of her childhood.

On July 18, 1992, Uptown released *What's the 411?* That summer, the album's debut single, "You Remind Me" was released on the radio airwaves. On *Billboard*'s Hot 100 Singles Chart, it eventually peaked at number twenty-nine, but it climbed to number one on *Billboard*'s R&B singles chart.

The album's first single was followed up that fall with "Real Love," which fared even better, becoming Blige's second number one on the R&B singles charts—and number seven on the Top 10 pop singles. Eventually, both singles were also certified **gold**.

Crowned

More *411* singles followed into 1993, including "Love No Limit," "Reminisce," and a **cover** of Chaka Khan's "Sweet Thing." By the end of the year, *What's the 411?* had sold three million copies, and Mary had been crowned "The Queen of Hip-Hop Soul." The album's success spun off a **remix** album released in December of 1993, which extended the radio life of the *411* singles all the way into 1994, while Mary prepared for her second album.

Meanwhile, Sean "Puffy" Combs (who was calling himself Puff Daddy by now) helped Blige fine-tune her voice and create an image for herself. Although Combs had left Uptown to create his own label, Bad Boy Entertainment, he took on the role of executive producer for Mary's next album, *My Life*, which was released in November 1994. This album was sadder, moodier, less upbeat than Mary's first album. Mary hadn't written the songs for her first album, but this time around, she did much of the writing. The songs were honest expressions of the bitter pain and dark depression she had experienced in life. Mary's voice might not have been spectacular—but her brutal honesty made her stand out from other musicians. Suddenly, she had a loyal following of fans.

Mary was taken aback by the reaction to her honesty. She was flattered, of course, but even more she was humbled—and for her fans' sakes, she was inspired to begin searching for the personal answers she needed to put her life together. She told UnderGroundOnline:

"After the *My Life* album there was a moment when I put it on wax, there were so many people that spoke to me or wrote me about that album and how they identified with that album and my suicidal pain.

For Mary's first album, *What's the 411?*, she worked with one of the up-and-comers of the music world, Sean "Puffy" Combs. The title refers to Mary's former career as a directory assistance operator. The album's success earned her the title "Queen of Hip-Hop Soul."

I didn't want them to go through those suicidal pains, so I wanted to get myself together so that we could all get ourselves together. I can't force things down people's throats but what I can do is try to fix Mary. **"**

The album's first single, "Be Happy," peaked at number twenty-nine on *Billboard*'s Hot 100, and then it shot up to number six on the R&B

My Life was all Mary—her pain, her depression, her honesty. And the fans loved it. She had written most of the songs on the album, and fans let her know they could identify with her music and her pain, a responsibility Mary takes seriously.

singles chart. In early 1995, it was followed up with a cover of Rose Royce's "I'm Goin' Down," as well as "You Bring Me Joy" and "I Love You." The entire album proved to be a multi-**platinum** success story, selling three million copies.

Bitterness in the Midst of Success

In spite of her growing fame, Blige was still struggling with the pain and anger that had followed her all the way from the Projects. As she struggled to deal with her new life as a music star, with all its demands, she also struggled to cope with bitter personal problems: her relationship with K-Ci had turned abusive, and Mary was drowning in multiple bouts of drug addiction, alcoholism, and depression. As so often

Along with a growing music career came love for Mary and K-Ci Hailey (left) of the group Jodeci. Sadly, theirs was an abusive relationship, and Mary often looked for comfort in drugs and alcohol. She got a reputation for being "difficult."

happens, her rage and anguish came out sideways; instead of tackling her problems head on, she gained a reputation for being difficult and moody, the sort of woman with whom no one enjoys working.

But Mary kept going with an angry courage that refused to give up. She poured all her bitterness and pain into her music.

Building a Career

Later in 1995, Mary took on several projects besides her own albums. She recorded a cover of Aretha Franklin's classic "(You Make Me Feel Like A) Natural Woman" for the soundtrack to the hit Fox series, *New York Undercover*, and she also created "Everyday It Rains" for the soundtrack to the hip-hop film, *The Show*. A few months later, she recorded a song written and produced by Babyface, "Not Gon' Cry," for the soundtrack of the motion picture, *Waiting to Exhale*; the soundtrack also featured several big names, including Whitney Houston, TLC, Brandy, and Toni Braxton. Mary's song made it all the way to number two.

She also performed a hit duet with rapper Method Man on his song, "I'll Be There For You/You're All I Need To Get By" (which **sampled** Marvin Gaye and Tammi Terrell's 1968 single, "You're All I Need to Get By"). In early 1996, Mary won her first Grammy: the Best Rap Vocal Performance by a Duo or Group for her collaboration with Method Man.

Going Solo

Mary's next album was made without any help from Combs or Andre Harrell. Combs was concentrating on the success of Notorious B.I.G., and Harrell had left Uptown to take over Motown Records. But Mary proved she had what it took to make it on her own, without the support of her **mentors**. She became her own executive producer, with the power to bring in the big names she needed to make her music shine.

In April 1997, MCA Records released Mary's third studio album, *Share My World*. To take Puff Daddy's place, a group of high-profile individuals had been recruited to produce the album, including Jimmy Jan, Terry Lewis, Chucky Thompson, R. Kelly, Babyface, and Rodney Jerkins. Mary's new album debuted at number one on *Billboard*'s Top 200 Albums Chart, and it also produced four hit singles: "Love Is All We Need" (featuring Nas), "I Can Love You" (featuring Lil Kim),

In 1995, Mary recorded songs for television and movie sound-tracks. She also recorded a hit song with rapper Method Man. Ten years later, they reteamed to perform the duet at the BET Silver Anniversary Celebration.

"Everything," and "Seven Days." The album went triple platinum and sold five million worldwide. And by early 1998, the album had earned Mary an American Music Award for Favorite Album—Soul/Rhythm & Blues. A few months later, in the summer of 1998, she embarked on

"I'll Be There for You/You're All I Need to Get By," Mary's hit duet with Method Man, brought the singer her first Grammy Award—Best Rap Vocal Performance by a Duo or Group—in February 1996.

the Share My World tour, which resulted in a gold-certified live album released later that year, titled simply *The Tour*.

Mary's career kept on rolling, full steam ahead. In August 1999, her fourth studio album, *Mary*, was released. The album was a departure from her usual hip-hop influenced sound; instead, it featured songs that sounded a little like the soul music of the 1970s and 1980s. The album also included a bevy of high-profile guests: Aretha Franklin (who sang a duet with Mary called "Don't Waste Your Time"), Elton John (who played keys on "Deep Inside," which featured a sample of his 1970s hit "Benny and the Jets"), Eric Clapton (who played guitar on "Give Me You"), and Lauryn Hill (who wrote, produced, and sang background on "All That I Can Say"). Mary also recorded a duet with George Michael called "As," which is included on the album's United Kingdom version. However, MCA left it out of the American album, since the record label felt that George Michael was too **controversial** and too openly homosexual to do Mary's career any good in the United States.

At the end of 1999, the *Mary* album was re-released as a double disc set. The second disc was enhanced with the videos for the singles "All That I Can Say" and "Deep Inside." The disc also included two bonus tracks: "Sincerity" (featuring Nas and DMX) and "Confrontation." Critics loved the album and it went double platinum, but it didn't sell quite as well as Mary's earlier albums. Mary, however, had learned to be not only a musician but a businesswoman; she and MCA tapped into the club market by issuing club-friendly dance remixes of the *Mary* singles. Mary scored a number-one hit on *Billboard*'s Dance Chart with "Your Child," which topped the chart for one week in October 2000.

That same year, Mary released the overseas-only compilation, *Ballads*, which featured the best of her ballad material. She also had a hit duet with Wyclef Jean, called "911," which was featured on his album *The Eclectic: 2 Sides II a Book*.

Her Own Style

By this time, Mary had created a unique sound, as well as a look that was all her own. While other female musicians tended to go for the ultra-glamorous, ultra-sexy look, Mary's fashion sense was true to her roots. Both her sound and her look came to be known as "ghetto fabulous," a glittery, polished upgrade of what everyone in the

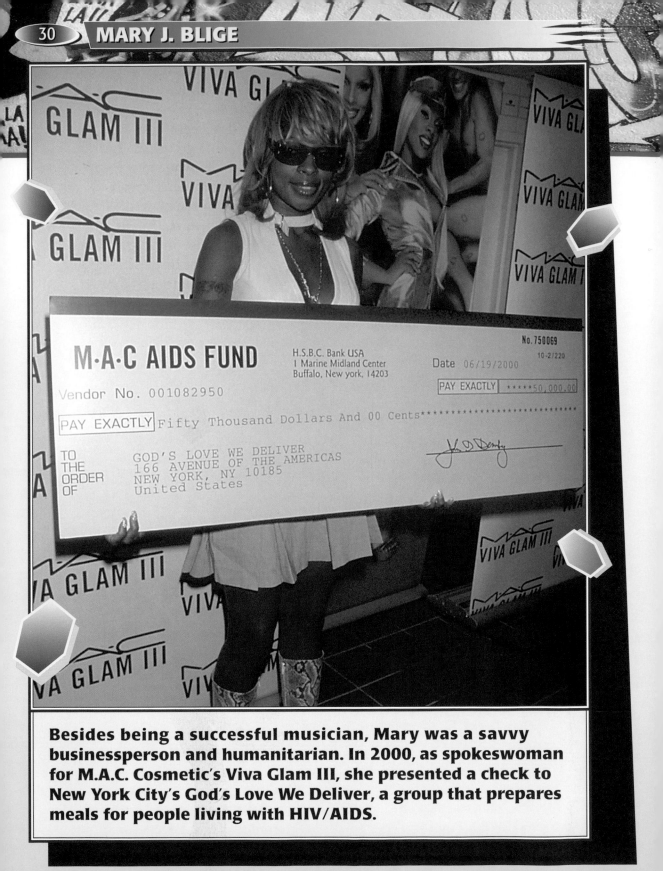

Besides being a successful musician, Mary was a savvy businessperson and humanitarian. In 2000, as spokeswoman for M.A.C. Cosmetic's Viva Glam III, she presented a check to New York City's God's Love We Deliver, a group that prepares meals for people living with HIV/AIDS.

"hood" was wearing and rapping. Urban black woman could easily identify with her.

Her fans respected that honesty; it made them feel they weren't all alone. Her songs were the voice of all the little girls growing up in the ghetto, the ones whose daddies left them, the ones who got pregnant because they wanted to know they were loved, the ones who grew up and became women who put up with abuse from their men because they didn't know how to find what would make them really happy.

Mary was also putting up with a lot of nonsense in her personal life—but in her music, she sang out loud and clear for the truth. When you speak the truth, no matter how ugly, sooner or later good comes from it. The Bible says, "The truth shall set you free."

Freedom was coming Mary's way.

Mary knew she couldn't go on using drugs and alcohol to hide her pain and anger. Her reputation and career had suffered because of it. She didn't know how to change; she just knew it was something she had to do.

3

No More Drama

Things couldn't go on like this much longer for Mary. She couldn't keep drinking and using drugs and still keep her professional life afloat. Even more important, sooner or later, if she didn't take better care of herself, her talent and creativity would begin to suffer as well. Mary knew things had to change—but she didn't know how to make that happen.

Hitting Bottom

Meanwhile, Mary's tough style didn't rub everyone the right way, particularly the media. She gained a reputation for being moody, frequently late, and extremely demanding. Mary *was* troubled and angry—but that reality meshed well with the image Puff Daddy had created for her. From the very beginning, he had encouraged her to express herself, both on stage and on her albums, with a raw angry emotion. Her real-life moodiness only made her true fans more sympathetic.

Mary told *The Guardian*:

> **I had no idea that my personal pain would create such a big fanbase. Everything that was bringing me down was everything that rose me up. From a business standpoint, that is. I was still down in my personal life. All the money and fame in the world couldn't change what was going on in my heart. That's how messed up I was, and how depressed I was.**

No matter what her fans thought, though, Mary knew the truth: her drug and alcohol consumption was a problem. She had a serious car accident as result of drunk driving. She was sometimes too high or too drunk for photo sessions. She told *The Guardian*:

> **I was drinking, I was doing drugs heavy, so I couldn't even feel or see anything, and that made it all right for the moment, until I had to come down and go look for some more. But at the end of the day, it depressed me. . . .**

As a result of her substance abuse, she was frequently late for rehearsals, tour dates, and interviews. She snapped at the people around her; she lost her temper a lot. People thought she was just plain rude. Truth was, Mary was struggling to make sense of her life—but it looked as though she were losing the battle. Years later, she told *Essence*:

> **Everyone was making decisions about me and what I should be doing, but I didn't necessarily agree with everything, so I wouldn't do things. The whole business wasn't as glamorous as it appeared to be on the outside.**

Steve Lucas, who became Mary's co-manager after she toured with two of his acts, Father MC and Jodeci, gave her professional advice during this rough period in her life. He also spoke out on her behalf in an interview with *Essence*:

> **When an artist's debut album sells millions of records, you'd better believe that things will fall**

Mary was too honest and not honest enough. She couldn't win. She yelled at people, skipped interviews. Some began to believe that was the *real* Mary J. Blige. She knew better, and she worked hard to change other's opinions about her, and hers about herself.

between the cracks if the team around the artist isn't tight. Mary got an undeserved bad rap because of what was going on around her—the confusion, the lack of organization. When you communicate honestly with Mary, there aren't any problems. She's willing to cooperate and do whatever it takes to be successful. She's basically a very sweet, humble person.**"**

Mary felt like she couldn't win. When she first became a star, music critics had praised her genuineness, saying that she was a true role model for the hip-hop generation. But now her critics were complaining that she wasn't sophisticated enough. She was *too* real. Some people didn't like her trademark combat boots. Others complained that her voice was too rough. Everyone seemed to have an opinion about who Mary should be and how she should look.

Mary told *Essence* that when she first became famous,

"I was like, 'Oh, I got this.' But I really didn't have it, because I didn't have my temper under control. I was angry, because it seemed like people were picking on me, and I could do nothing about it. . . . I was irritated."

Meanwhile, Mary's personal life was falling apart at the seams. K-Ci publicly humiliated her; rumor had it that privately things were even worse. Like a kid acting out when she's angry with her parents, Mary's misbehavior was just another way her hurt and rage were coming out sideways—and in the end, she was the one she was hurting most.

A New Life

In 2000, Mary put her self-destructive romantic relationships behind her and launched into a far more healthy relationship with record industry executive Martin Kendu Isaacs. Kendu helped Mary overcome her dependency on drugs and alcohol. At first, Mary turned to food as substitute for the drugs and alcohol she was denying herself. She put on a good deal of weight (which her critics were quick to point out), but Mary was getting her life in shape. In 2001, she began exercising and eating healthy; she lost forty pounds, but even better, she was finally happy with herself.

In 2000, Mary took control of Mary. With the help of record executive Martin Kendu Isaacs, she kicked abusive relationships, drugs, and alcohol. With two awards at the *Soul Train* Music Awards, including Female Entertainer of the Year, her career was also on the rebound.

Everything Mary went through made her identify even more with her fans, the people who responded so openly to her own challenges and pain. She told *The Guardian*:

❝**The world is in pain. Right now, there's a fat girl at home, eating potato chips and . . . she thinks she's**

In 2003, Mary and Kendu Isaacs, the man she credits with helping her overcome her self-destructive behavior, were married. She was attracted by his relationships with his family and with God. Mary wanted that kind of life as well.

nothing because the television says you have to be skinny to be beautiful. Society wants to make you think you don't even have a place on the earth.

Mary had finally learned that she had her own special place on earth. She was no longer depending on drugs or a man to make her feel better. As a result, she was finally free to have a healthy and healing relationship with a man. Mary and Kendu were married on December 7, 2003. Mary became the stepmother to Kendu's three children, and the couple began thinking about having more children as well.

Mary described to *The Guardian* one way her relationship with Kendu helped her to move away from her destructive habits:

"When you can see better, you want better. And you know, my husband, he had something better. He had a mom that raised him, he had a father that raised him. He had a family unit. He had sisters and brothers that weren't jealous of him. He didn't have to fight them. He had beautiful things in him, and he was already a Christian when I met him. When I saw his life, that's the life I wanted."

Mary concluded the interview with a summary of her new way of looking at herself: "I believe what God says about me. He says that I'm beautiful, I'm strong, I'm a good woman, I have love in my heart, I can be fat or skinny . . . I can do whatever I want."

Going Strong

Meanwhile, Mary's professional life was also doing well. In the summer of 2001, MCA released Mary's fifth studio album, *No More Drama*. The album was an anthem of joy to her new attitude on life. Its first single, "Family Affair," produced by Dr. Dre, became Mary's first number-one song on *Billboard*'s Hot 100 Singles Chart, where it stayed for six consecutive weeks. Ultimately, it was one of the year's biggest songs, and the biggest hit so far in Mary's career. "Family Affair" was followed by another top-20 single, which sampled the famous piano theme to the daytime drama *The Young and the Restless*.

Although the singles were big hits, MCA wasn't pleased with the entire album's sales, so they repackaged and re-released it early in 2002.

Sales shot up, and the album went on to be certified double platinum, selling four million worldwide. Mary won her second Grammy for the song "He Think I Don't Know."

Back with Puff Daddy

In August 2003, Mary's sixth album, *Love & Life*, was released by Geffen Records (which had absorbed MCA). Puff Daddy (now called

NO MORE DRAMA

In 2001, with her life now under control, Mary released the album *No More Drama*. Unlike some of her albums of the past, this one was joyful, reflecting the newfound happiness of her personal life.

P. Diddy) and Mary reunited for this album and collaborated on the production.

However, Mary and Diddy often butted heads during the album's production. In the end, the album showed the effects of their struggles. Although it eventually went platinum, both critics and fans thought it was far from being either Mary's or Diddy's best work. Once the project was completed, the two decided to again part company.

Mary had learned not to doubt her own instincts. She knew that life will always have its ups and downs—but that deep down, her sense of who she is could remain stable. She told *Essence*: "You know I am finally happy with myself. I have found some peace of mind. And I've finally realized that I have God in my life. So I know I'm never really alone.

Mary performs live during the "Love & Life" tour in 2004. The *Love & Life* album was received with less than enthusiastic criticism. Mary realized that she hadn't been totally honest with her fans on the album—there had been "too many cooks in the kitchen"—and she vowed not to let that happen again.

4

Breakthrough

hen *Love & Life* failed to live up to expectations, critics speculated that happiness didn't agree with Mary J. Blige's music. They wondered if her personal well-being meant that her songs had lost their bittersweet edge. But Mary knew better. She gave herself time to heal. Working with P. Diddy again had confused her, but her life was finally on track.

She told UnderGroundOnline:

"I kind of fell into a slump and people didn't know what was going to happen. People weren't sure if I was done. They were guessing. When you are in a healing process, you get into a dark area called confusion. During the *Love & Life* album there was a lot of confusion and no one really knew what I was doing, and there was too many

cooks in the kitchen. When you go with your heart you lose a lot of people because, in my heart, I had to get well, but then you have Puffy saying we needed to make people dance and I didn't know that. I think my fans appreciate it more when I give them the raw and real Mary."

In an MTV interview, Mary went into more details about what had happened with *Love & Life*:

"When we put the *Love & Life* album out, it was a dessert, because I don't believe I was being as honest with my fans as I normally am. I wasn't being honest because I had record company people in my life saying, 'No, don't sing with that much emotion. Don't do this, don't do that.' I'm thinking, 'Oh, OK. Don't do that? OK.' Turns out, that little feeling you get inside of you saying, 'Don't do it'—I didn't listen to it. The people are not stupid. They know when I'm for real and they know when I'm being pushed for something else."

Mary had learned her lesson: next time around, she would be true to herself.

Being True to Mary

Rumors circulated in the summer of 2005 that Mary's next release would be a greatest-hits **retrospective** titled *Reminisce*. But Mary and her label took everyone by surprise when they announced that instead an album of brand-new material was on its way. In December, Geffen released Mary's seventh studio album, *The Breakthrough*.

The album's uplifting lyrics were different from Mary's earlier bitterness and anger. But they were honest. They expressed what was really going on in her life—and Mary wasn't about to pretend otherwise. She told *The Scotsman*, "I've been through hell, and I'm not going through hell for you or anybody on planet Earth any more." She added,

"When you grow up in a place where people are rejecting you and you experience abuse, your self-esteem is all screwed up from the start. I'm mean and hateful, because my mom and dad were mean and hateful to me. But eventually I realized that I had to break the destructive cycle I was in. . . .

A lot of soul is about 'My man done me wrong' and all that. My mother played those songs over and over, drumming the idea into her head: 'I'm a victim, I'm a victim.' But I'm sick of being a victim. That's over. I'm the victor now. "

Mary was back on top of things with the December 2005 release of *Breakthrough*. In January 2006, she was ready to sign copies of her CD for the fans who had stood by her through it all.

Critics and fans alike were pleased with the new album, proving that Mary was right: it wasn't misery that her music needed; it was integrity. She told UnderGroundOnline: "I didn't have the distractions with this one and I went totally crazy with what was going on in my heart because I didn't want to let them down again." She went into even more detail with MTV:

> **The Breakthrough is about getting to or going to a place where we fear the most. Going to a place where people are gonna talk about us. . . . This album is basically Mary J. Blige not being what everybody else wanted her to be. You either like this or you don't. This is about making a choice to survive.**

The album's lead-off single, "Be Without You," raced up both the R&B and pop singles charts, topping the R&B chart for a record-breaking fifteen consecutive weeks. Meanwhile, the album simultaneously debuted at number-one on both the R&B and Top-200 albums charts. In its first week, it sold more than 700,000 copies, the biggest first-week sales for an R&B solo female artist in Sound Scan history, the fifth-largest first-week sales for a female artist, and the fourth-largest debut of the 2005. It soon went platinum.

The album included a surprise collaboration: Mary and U2's Bono singing a duet of the 1992 hit "One." Mary told *The Guardian* that she had enjoyed working with Bono. "The chemistry between us was incredible. . . . There's something special about this song. It's not my usual kind of music, but it just blew me away." Mary's unique style breathed new passion and anger into the lyrics: "I can't be holding on/To what you got/When all you got is hurt."

Creativity in Blossom

In December 2005, word spread that Mary's creativity was blossoming in more ways than one: she had landed the starring role in an MTV film on Nina Simone. In fact, the film's writer, Cynthia Mort personally targeted Mary for the role. She felt Mary was the perfect person to bring Simone to life.

Nina Simone was an African American musician whose **repertoire** ranged from jazz to African music, from blues to **gospel**, from classical music to folk songs from around the world. Although Nina's fans called

One of the biggest surprises on *Breakthrough* was Mary's duet with Bono on U2's megahit "One." In 2006, Mary, Bono, and U2 wowed the crowd when they performed the song at the 48th Annual Grammy Awards.

her the "High Priestess of Soul," she was also often misunderstood. In the 1960s, she was outspoken on behalf of **civil rights**. Eventually, she fled the United States, saying that she was a victim of prejudice and racism. She died in France in 2003. Without a doubt, Mary J. Blige has the passion to bring to life Nina Simone's frustration, talent, and integrity.

This was not Mary's first acting experience. In 1998, she had played Ola Mae on the *Jamie Foxx Show*, portraying a preacher's daughter who wanted to sing more than gospel music. In 2001, Mary played Mrs. Butler in the independent feature film, *Prison Song*, starring rapper Q-Tip. Mary particularly identified with this role, since it mirrored parts of her own family life. The same year, Mary made a **cameo** appearance on the Lifetime network series, *Strong Medicine*, where she played Simone Fellows, a lead singer who is sick but refuses to seek help. In 2004, Mary starred in her first off-Broadway play, *The Exonerated*, which told the stories of real death-row inmates. Blige portrayed Sunny Jacobs, a woman who spent twenty years in prison for a crime she didn't commit.

Mary has expanded her career to include acting. In 2001, she appeared on the television show *Strong Medicine*, with series regular Rosa Blasi (left). She will also appear in a project about Nina Simone, the "High Priestess of Soul."

As Mary put her life together, she also launched another new enterprise: her own record label, MJB. She signed on many of the artists who had collaborated with her on previous projects, as well as many new artists. Mary was proud of the talent she had brought together—and she was excited about the opportunities her own label gave her to help build the music world, especially the world of hip-hop.

With so many accomplishments now under her belt, Mary was in good place as she looked forward. She told MTV her advice for others who were struggling to get ahead:

"As a human being, no matter how cool you are, you still are goofy sometimes, you still are corny sometimes and don't care what people say about it. People are always gonna have something to say. Just be who you are."

Now that Mary had put her personal demons to rest, she was also free to reach out to others with new strength and authority.

Mary could always count on her fans to stand by her, through thick and thin. So she gives back to the world through her many charitable activities, including work with a dental care outreach program, Crest Healthy Smiles.

5

Journey of Love

"One life/But we're not the same/ We get to carry each other." These words from the U2 song "One," which Mary performed with Bono, summarizes the philosophy that inspires Mary to reach out to others. Her willingness to be vulnerable and honest allows her to cross the differences that lie between human beings—and offer her strength to those who are weaker.

In an interview with ASCAP, Mary explained what inspires her to keep on being the best she can be for the sake of others:

"It's not easy, but the bottom line is: I'm created from a higher power that's bigger than people, you know what I mean? I can't do anything other than try to do the best that I can so that when this is all over for me, I go to a place that the Creator created for me just for being obedient. And it's not easy. It's not easy because for me the choice that I made is to want to be a better person because it hurts too much to be a terrible person. So this is all for me and for God."

Mary's Charities

Mary has racked up an impressive array of good works. For example, she performed with Whitney Houston in the Diva's Life concert to benefit music education in public schools. She also took part in the NetAid concert with Wyclef Jean. (NetAid is an organization that seeks to educate young people about global poverty and provide opportunities for them to take concrete actions that will make a difference in the lives of the world's poor.) Mary has teamed up with Wyclef Jean for another cause as well: they work together to donate musical instruments to underprivileged children. What's more, she has worked with Reverend Al Sharpton, Martin Luther King III, and Russell Simmons on Rap the Vote, encouraging urban youth to vote. Her work on behalf of AIDS charities and research has also earned her praise. *Rolling Stone* gave her the magazine's Do Something Award, and she was awarded the Patrick Lippert Award from Rock the Vote.

For Mary, charity is more than just giving money. Sharing her life with honesty and openness is essential to her philosophy of giving. She explained to ASCAP:

"People are like, why do you let people get so personal in your life? Why not? I mean, they see it when they see me and buy the records. Why would I put a bunch of stuff on there that later doesn't match up with who I am? Then I'm a fraud. So the knowledge is . . . the charity."

Mary's **candor** about her personal life gives her the opportunity to speak just as frankly to her fans' lives. At a concert in the United Kingdom, for instance, she lectured the audience about their responsibilities to their children. "Take care of the children NOW!" she commanded her fans. "Some of y'all might not like what I'm saying," she continued, "but I DON'T CARE!"

In 2000, Mary was involved with Rap the Vote 2000, a program to increase political awareness among young, black youth. Here, Mary is shown with (left to right) Reverend Al Sharpton, Martin Luther King III, and Russell Simmons.

Mary speaks often about spiritual issues; she credits God with her new, healthier approach to life. But because she exposes her own pain and failure, she never comes across as smug or holier than thou. She sees her music as far more than a career. For her, it's a ministry. In an interview with UnderGroundOnline, she admitted that her sense of responsibility to her fans can be exhausting—and yet it's worth the effort.

"When someone comes to me and says that I've saved their lives—that has kept me doing this. . . . I was doing an interview a couple of weeks ago where fans were calling in and a girl said, 'Mary, I'm glad you are back but where were you when I needed you?' That moved me and told me it was bigger than me. But it gets hard. You have no idea how humbling that is. . . . I can't cure anyone but because God gave me the ability to speak on my life and make it a ministry."

Despite the tribulations of her life and career, Mary J. Blige has come out a winner. Her music has been called groundbreaking, and her inspiration has been important to many who have heard her lyrics and found in them a common bond with the musician.

Making a Mark

Mary has touched the world in many ways. Since emerging on the music scene in 1992, she has laid a new path for other female artists to follow, including Aaliyah, Beyoncé, Amerie, Alicia Keys, Lil' Mo, Nicole Wray, Ashanti, Tweet, P!nk, Lauryn Hill, and Keyshia Cole. She wasn't the first female artist to mix hip-hop and soul, but her combination of hip-hop street beats and soulful vocals was truly groundbreaking. Her success was also instrumental in building the careers of P. Diddy, as well as rappers such as Notorious B.I.G. and Busta Rhymes, as well as R&B singer-songwriter Faith Evans. Mary has earned the respect of her peers and elders, both in and outside of her own genre.

In her interview with ASCAP, Mary encouraged others to embark on their own journeys of love and make a difference to the world around them. She said:

"For so long we have been told that we don't have any control over our destiny, but we do. We have control of our destiny. We were created in the image of a God who is the head spirit of our spirits. And we need to know that we have so much power that flows through us that we can choose. We've been given a free will to live as we please. So choose what you want. . . . I chose being positive because I've been on the negative side for too long. So make your choice. That's the bottom line, you have a choice."

1970s Hip-hop is born in the Bronx, New York.

1971 Mary J. Blige is born on January 11 in the Bronx, New York.

1989 Signs with Uptown Records.

1992 Releases her debut album, *What's the 411?*

1994 Sean "Puffy" Combs produces *My Life*, Mary's second album.

1995 Covers Aretha Franklin's "(You Make Me Feel Like A) Natural Woman."

1996 Wins her first Grammy.

1998 Wins American Music Award.

Plays Ola Mae on the *Jamie Foxx Show*.

1999 Records *Mary*, which features Aretha Franklin, Elton John, Eric Clapton, and Lauryn Hill.

2000 Begins relationship with Martin Kendu Isaacs.

2001 Appears in the film *Prison Song*.

2002 Performs an emotional rendition of "No More Drama" on the Grammy Awards.

2003 Marries Martin Kendu Isaacs.

2004 Appears in her first off-Broadway play, *The Exonerated*.

2005 Releases critically acclaimed and commercially successful album *The Breakthrough*.

Lands the title role in MTV's film about Nina Simone.

2006 Appears on the hit television show *Dancing with the Stars*.

Discography
Albums
1992   *What's the 411?*
1993   *What's the 411? Remix*
1994   *My Life*
1997   *Share My World*
1998   *The Tour*
1999   *Mary*
2001   *No More Drama*
2002   *Dance for Me*
2003   *Love & Life*
2005   *The Breakthrough*

Number-one Singles
1992   "You Remind Me"; "Real Love"
1995   "You Bring Me Joy"
1996   "Not Gon' Cry"
1997   "Love Is All We Need" (with Nas)
2000   "Your Child"; "Confrontation"
2001   "Family Affair"; "Dance for Me"
2002   "No More Drama"
2003   "Love
2005   "Be Without You"

Selected Television Appearances
1993   *Saturday Night Live*
1994   *The Word*
1995   *New York Undercover*
1997   *Late Show with David Letterman*; *The Chris Rock Show*
1998   *The Jamie Foxx Show*
1999   *Moesha*
2001   *America the Beautiful*; *Intimate Portrait: Mary J. Blige*; *Prison Song*; *Strong Medicine*; *The 2nd Annual Women Rock! Girls and Guitars*; *The Tonight Show with Jay Leno*

2003   *The 9th Annual Walk of Fame Honoring Aretha Franklin*; *VH1Diva Duets*; *The Oprah Winfrey Show*

2004   *And You Don't Stop: 30 Years of Hip-Hop*; *Fahrenheit 9/11: A Movement in Time*; *Genius: A Night for Ray Charles*; *Ellen: The Ellen DeGeneres Show*

2005   *Shelter from the Storm: A Concert for the Gulf Coast*; *Tsunami Aid: A Concert of Hope*; *25 Strong: The BET Silver Anniversary Special*; *The Tyra Banks Show*; *Tavis Smiley*; *Top of the Pops*; *The View*

2006   *Dancing with the Stars*; *The Tonight Show with Jay Leno*; *The Oprah Winfrey Show*

Film
2007   Untitled Nina Simone Project

Video
2000   *It's Only Rock 'n' Roll*

2001   *MTV20: Jams*

2004   *Mary J. Blige: Queen of Hip Hop Soul*; *The Notorious B.I.G.: Ready to Die—The Remaster*

2005   *The Music of* Shark Tale

Awards
1993   New York Music Awards: Best Debut R&B Artist of the Year; Best R&B Album; Rising Star Award; *Soul Train* Awards: Best New Artist; Best R&B Soul Singer

1994   Source Awards: R&B Artist of the Year

1995   Source Awards: R&B Artist of the Year; *Billboard* Music Awards: R&B Album of the Year; Soul Train Lady of Soul Awards: Best Video

1996   *Soul Train* Lady of Soul Awards: Best Single by Solo Artist; Grammy Awards: Best Performance by a Duo or Group; *Soul Train* Awards: Album of the Year—Female

1998   American Music Awards: Favorite Album—Soul/R&B; Soul Train Lady of Soul Awards: R&B Soul Album of the Year

1999   New York Chapter of the Recording Academy: Heroes Award; Sister Inter-Generational Award: You're My Sis Award

2000   *Soul Train* Awards: Best R&B Soul Album—Female; Soul Train Lady of Soul Awards: R&B/Soul or Rap Song of the Year; R&B/Soul Album of the Year

2001   BET Awards: Best Female R&B Artist

2002   MTV Video Music Awards: Best R&B Video

2003   American Music Awards: Favorite Hip-Hop/R&B Female Artist; Grammy Awards: Best Female R&B Performance; *Soul Train* Awards: Female R&B Soul Album

2004   Grammy Awards: Best Pop Collaboration with Vocals

2005   *Vibe* Awards: Legend Award

Books

Hinds, P. Mignon, and Susan L. Taylor. *50 of the Most Inspiring African-Americans.* New York: Essence Books, 2005.

Knight, Judson, and Allison McNeill. *Parents Aren't Supposed to Like It: Rock & Other Pop Musicians of Today.* Detroit, Mich.: UXL, 2002.

Samuels, Allison, and Michele Wood. *Christmas Soul: African American Holiday Stories.* New York: Jump at the Sun/Hyperion Books for Children, 2001.

VIBE. *Hip-Hop Divas.* New York: Three Rivers Press, 2001.

Magazines

Bernstein, Jacob. "Proud Mary." *WWD*, December 12, 2005.

Chappell, Kevin. "The New Mary J. Blige Tells How Drugs and Attitude Almost Ruined Her Sizzling Career." *Ebony*, January 1, 1998.

Chappell, Kevin. "Mary J. Blige's Tearful Plea: 'I've Got to Be Me.'" *Ebony*, October 1, 2003.

Dunn, Jancee. "Mary J. Blige on Fear and Clothing." *W*, October 1, 2004.

Gregory, Deborah. "Proud Mary." *Essence*, March 1, 1995.

Samuels, Allison. "Much Obliged: Teary-Voiced Mary J. Blige is Grateful." *Newsweek*, August 25, 2003.

Whetstone, Muriel L. "Goin' Down and Up with Mary J. Blige." *Ebony*, October 1, 1995.

Web Sites

"The Continuing Drama of Mary J. Blige"
www.rollingstone.com/news/story/9447919

Mary J. Blige
www.maryjblige.com

Mary J. Blige
www.starpulse.com/Music/Blige,_Mary_J.

Rock on the Net: Mary J. Blige
www.rockonthenet.com/artists-b/maryjblige_main.htm

affirmation—a positive statement.

brazen—showing or expressing boldness and complete lack of shame.

cameo—a single, brief appearance by a distinguished actor in a film or television program.

candor—honesty or directness.

civil rights—the basic rights that all individuals should have.

controversial—provoking strong disagreement or disapproval.

cover—to record a new version of a song that was first sung by another performer.

debut—done for the first time.

democratic—characterized by equal participation in government or in the decision-making process of a group or organization.

DJ—someone who plays recorded music for the entertainment of others; disc jockey.

dubbed—remixed records to bring some instruments into the foreground and cause others to echo.

gold—signifying that an album has sold 500,000 copies.

gospel—highly emotional evangelical vocal music that originated among African American Christians in the southern United States.

impromptu—spur of the moment.

improvised—made up without preparation.

marginalized—prevented from having attention or power.

mentors—more experienced people who help guide someone who is not as experienced.

mixer—a machine that adjusts and combines multiple inputs to create a single output.

platinum—signifying that a single has sold one million copies, or that an album or CD has sold two million copies.

R&B—rhythm and blues; a mixture of jazz and blues.

reggae—popular music, originally from Jamaica, that combines elements of rock, calypso, and soul.

remix—to produce a new version of a piece of music by altering the emphasis of the sound and adding new tracks.

repertoire—the range of techniques, abilities, or skills that someone has.

retrospective—containing examples of work from different periods of an individual's life.

sampled—used a segment of another person's music as part of one's own.

sociologists—scientists who study society, social relationships, and social institutions.

soul—music that originated in African American gospel singing and is characterized by strong feeling and earthiness.

Terrell Brown believes in the power of language to shape the world. He hopes to use his writing to encourage young people to learn to value themselves and make positive choices, as Mary J. Blige did. Terrell lives in upstate New York with his family and five pet goats.

Picture Credits

page

2: Marcocchi Giulio/SIPA

8: Zuma Press/Nancy Kaszerman

11: Reuters/Mike Segar

13: Zuma Press/Aviv Small

14: Tina Paul/WENN

15: Gary James/WENN

16: KRT/Olivier Douliery

18: MTV Studios/Zuma Press

21: UPI/Robin Platzer

23: Zuma Press/Aviv Small

24: Zuma Press/Finn Frandsen/ Polfoto

25: Zuma Press/Toronto Star

27: Reuters/Mario Anzuoni

28: AFP/Jeff Haynes

30: Zuma Press/Nancy Kaszerman

32: Zuma Press/Roce/DAPR

35: Zuma Press/Rena Durham

37: Reuters/Gary Hershorn

38: PRNewsFoto/NMI

40: Michelle Feng/NMI

42: Zuma Press/Patty June Photo

45: Charley Gallay/London Entertainment/Splash News

47: Lester Cohen/WireImage

48: Zuma Press/Columbia TriStar TV

50: Feature Photo Service/Jeff Klein

53: UPI/Ezio Petersen

54: Michael Loccisano/FilmMagic

Front cover: Russ Elliot/AdMedia
Back cover: KRT/Oliver Douliery